POMEGRANATE SEEDS
& MISDEEDS

POMEGRANATE SEEDS & MISDEEDS

LYRA WREN

Indianapolis, Indiana

Lyra Wren
@poetrybylyra
linktr.ee/poetrybylyra

ISBN: 979-8-9915591-2-6

Edited by Maddie Portune

Cover and Book Design by Keller Makemson
@kmakemson.design
kmakemson.com

For those who were dragged into darkness
and learned to call it home.
For those who return in their own time,
changed, sovereign, whole.

The girl was born with too much empathy,
cursed with a bleeding heart.
The gods gave her beauty and love
and others granted her a gift for the arts.

Persephone showed her the difference
between godhood and girlhood
and how they sometimes look the same.

Hades taught her about life and death,
how grief is just love by another name.

She learned the power of motherhood from Demeter
and how to let your children go.
That even if you want to keep them,
they'll still find a way to grow.

"How do you carry the weight of these feelings?"
She asked. "Do the gods feel them too?"

We do.

"Even the gods?"

Even the gods,
Even the gods,
Even the gods,
They echoed.

Contents

Section I:
Persephone Speaks

LYRA WREN

My tale is told in one of two ways:

A young girl stolen away from mother,
imprisoned and forced to make hell her home.

A young goddess hungry for power,
who rejected her mother and all she'd ever known.

As in most tales told, the truth lies in between.
But regardless, I will be crowned
the victor in my own story.

POMEGRANATE SEEDS & MISDEEDS

They may call it naivety
but I was a wild thing.
Running in my mother's fields
and weaving daisy chains.

My mother shielded me so
I didn't know about the bad in this world.
I was free to love fiercely and explore endlessly.
To enjoy the entirety of my girlhood.

There was no way of knowing
how easily this peace could slip away.
But that's part of growing older —
you lose the innocence you now crave.

LYRA WREN

I ran through meadows,
chasing the sun,
where flowers bloomed
and time stood still.

My giggles, a melody in the breeze
untouched by what was to come.

The first time I touched a flower
and it wilted beneath my hand,
I feared the power inside of me.

Knowing my overprotective mother
would worry if she were to see,
I ran deep into the forest and
hid it under an old yew tree.

I spent hours tending to other flowers.
Flowers that grew with ease
with a mere touch of my finger.

I could have healed that flower if I tried
but instead, for days I snuck away to watch it die.
Petals falling and rotting in the heat of the sun.

Finally once it was nearly ash in my hand
I brought it back to life and did it all again.

Demeter harvested the land with gentle hands
while Kore held the scythe.
She and Death felt like long time friends.
Maybe she'd always been half girl, half knife.

POMEGRANATE SEEDS & MISDEEDS

Before him, I was only light.
Laughter in the meadows,
bare feet stained with pollen dust.

The world was soft.
My mother's arms wide as the sky,
and nothing ever ended.

I didn't know then
that even petals can bruise.

I cried out for my mother.
I cried out for my father.
I was pressed to the earth
and the rest was just noise.

POMEGRANATE SEEDS & MISDEEDS

Call it what it was:
A kidnapping or
an arranged marriage.
A choice taken from her.

Kore grew
to love him, she did.
But she wished it hadn't been like this.

LYRA WREN

The truth is, part of me wanted to leave.
To come into my power
and grow into the goddess queen
I knew I could be.

But, I miss my mother.
The girl I was before
cries out for her still.

POMEGRANATE SEEDS & MISDEEDS

They say he took me.
Dragged me beneath the earth
where sunlight dies and names are forgotten.

But they don't know that something in me
had already begun to rot.
Sweet things often do
when left too long in the sun.

He did not speak,
only looked at me like I was something familiar,
like he'd seen this hunger before.

And I, tired of innocence,
of being worshipped but never known,
took the pomegranate seeds
and let them stain my mouth red.

It is said that in my innocence
I didn't know what eating here meant.

It is said that I wanted to escape my mother
and my fate as Goddess of Spring.

It is said I slipped red rubies
beneath my lips for love.

Why must a girl's driving force
always be love or escapism?

POMEGRANATE SEEDS & MISDEEDS

Say what you will but
Kore knew what eating
in the Underworld meant.

She was no longer the naive girl
she'd been when she was taught this.
The girl who played with the nymphs
in her mother's fields.

She still held life in one hand but
the allure of the throne tempted her.
For so long, her choices had been taken.

No choice in being confined
to Demeter's fields.
No choice in being taken
by Hades into the Underworld.

She met Hades eyes and raised
six pomegranate seeds to her lips.
This choice would be hers.

The identity of Kore
did not fit around her skin anymore.
She is *girl* no longer.
Not a maiden in need of saving.

Part of her wants to linger in the past
but only ghosts of who she was remain.

Persephone, the Underworld murmured.
Persephone.

She answered: *Persephone will be my name.*

Had I not taken those seeds,
the name Kore may have faded until
I was unknown once more.

I miss how things used to be
but already I was changed.
Persephone, Queen of the Underworld:
that name held power.

Hades offered me a place in the mortal's memories.
Their voices tinged in fear and delight.
All will know my story.

Everyone wants to believe that I was simply naive
but I counted out those six seeds oh so carefully.
I placed each one intentionally on my tongue
and swallowed them down one by one.
Hades was triumphant, my mother dismayed
but in truth I was the one who emerged a victor that day.
I took the hand that fate dealt me and crowned myself
the Queen of Damnation for eternity.

I may have started out as a victim
but I sure as hell wouldn't stay one.

The gods of Olympus saw right through me.
Claiming that a floral maiden is all I'd ever be
but you saw me for what I was.

After all, I am a goddess too,
not just Demeter's daughter.
I'm just as hungry for power as the rest.

All I want is to be known
and you offered me *that* and a throne.

In his silence, I heard no cruelty.
Only a kind of loneliness
that mirrored something in me.

The gods above called it a cage
but they never saw how gently he looked at me.
How the dark was not empty
but full of things in bloom.

POMEGRANATE SEEDS & MISDEEDS

Oh sweet Persephone,

Even mortal women must break from
their mothers to become something new.
So when you peeled that pomegranate
and ate its seeds, did it taste of freedom?
Did the darkness offer you something
that springtime and light never could?
The gods always pegged you as one thing,
but not *him*. He recognized the duality
within you. He saw you and saw a queen.
I hear the nymphs cried for you and asked
if you were afraid. I hear thorns grew at
your feet and when your ichor bled into
the Underworld, you warned the gods
against a woman's contradictions and said,
it is *me* they should fear.

I no longer wear any chains
and this crown, I've claimed as mine.
Built from ash and bone
and the softness I did not leave behind.

I walk these halls and I am no prisoner
but a promise whispered between gods.
And when spring comes again
I will not return but I will rise.

Mother,

I'm sorry I became a thunderstorm
instead of a tranquil field of flowers.

I know you deserved more for a daughter
but this rage burns deeply in my blood.

Maybe I got it from my father.

LYRA WREN

Each spring, my mother hands me the sun
and watches me thaw until my skin beams.
She warms my hands between her own,
nurturing me as she nourishes her flowers.

The shadows of death still linger
in the petals that wilt when I walk by
but after many years, my mother does not fear this
and she always brings them back to life.

I know that soon I will return to Hades
and the earth and I will return to decay.
But for now, I lay my head in my mother's lap,
content with these warmer days.

Section II:
The Mortal Confesses

I think many girls feel a kinship with Persephone
because just like her we grit our teeth
and get our hands dirty.
Clawing our way through the walls
society tries to confine us in.

We are not meant to be poked and prodded at,
like pretty things to be placed on a pedestal
because beauty is not our best trait.

I know why Kore in all her rage
chose a kingdom of bone and grave,
taking on an entirely new name along with her reign.

There is a touch of chaos burning beneath our gentle eyes
and we despise those who try to snuff it out.

Girls will become goddesses through their own means
because we, too, are ravenous for better things.

Something feral is trapped behind my ribs,
ravenous for something more.
It threatens to consume me.
Is this how you felt, Kore?

As a child I lived more
and worried less about my looks
and the ways in which I was perceived.

Self-consciousness was a future
that I could not see.
Instead I ran around barefoot
– a wild girl with knotted hair,
and bruised knees.
I was allowed to just *be*.

Now all I do is stare at the mirror
and doubt the woman looking back at me.

POMEGRANATE SEEDS & MISDEEDS

If ghosts are real, you'll find them
haunting my childhood bedroom.
I am now a stranger in this place
I used to call my home.

My house lies in a cemetery
and there's no past to return to.
I'm not the same person anymore.

People said the girl was sunsoaked.
She was so warm and kind.
But in the name of people-pleasing
she was burning inside.

POMEGRANATE SEEDS & MISDEEDS

I'm sorry.
I wanted to stay gentle.
To remain a soft little girl.

I tried to have an open heart
but it just keeps bleeding.
Caused by a cruel world
and calloused hands.

I'm sorry for this rage
running through my blood.
I'm sorry that I've hurt
those who I have loved.

I'm sorry to the girls
who have been forced to survive
just in the hopes of staying alive.

I'm still searching for the girl I was.
The one who danced without thinking.
The one who believed the world was wide enough
for every dream she had.

I'm not trying to bring her back.
I'm just trying to understand
how she came to be me.

POMEGRANATE SEEDS & MISDEEDS

As a girl, I made myself smaller
when confronted with rage.
I couldn't help but be afraid of
this anger running through my own veins.

I thought this fire belonged to others.
Loud men, slamming doors and
mothers with mouths like storms
who never learned to soften.

It's alright
if you don't feel like spring today.
If the world is blooming when you are not.

There will be days when a winter's chill
settles into your bone marrow
and you can't crawl out of bed
but please remember,
even the earth rests between seasons.

POMEGRANATE SEEDS & MISDEEDS

They tell me to soften, to smile more,
 to make my rage small enough to swallow.

But I was not built to be quiet.
My blood sings in storms.

I am not sorry for the fire in my chest,
for the way my voice cuts through silence like a blade.

Let them call it too much.
Let them flinch.
I am not here to make them comfortable.

I am here to burn.

Not all monsters are to be feared.
Some are just women
who had to fight for too long.

Women with calloused hands and tired eyes.
Who learned to bare their teeth
before anyone allowed them to cry.

They were soft once. Like you.
They bent until they splintered.
And when no one came to save them,
they stitched themselves back together.

POMEGRANATE SEEDS & MISDEEDS

Deflower is such a cruel term
because she will continue to bloom
long after you are gone.

Her petals will not wilt
if they are plucked away by greedy hands
and her body is not yours to triumph.

You will never take away her ability
to build stronger roots
and blossom far brighter than before.

Rarely have I found love to be kind.
It is violent.
Even in its warmth, it burns.

I thought it would feel gentle
filling my chest
but the intensity of it
always has me gasping for breath.

I do not know how to love softly.
I am *always* all in.
It either consumes me
or I feel nothing.

POMEGRANATE SEEDS & MISDEEDS

Eat my heart like a pomegranate.
Love me so deeply and tear me to pieces.

Pry me open, messy and wanting,
desperately craving to be known.

The taste of me will stain
your lips and fingers red.
Will you still reach for me?

I will offer myself to you again and again
so please hold me with a tender touch
and soft hands.

Love me through the chaos
of picking me apart.

LYRA WREN

There was a time I ran
with my heart in my hands
and the stars felt like old friends
whispering my name.

But time has a way of taking,
slowly and quietly then
all at once without asking.

Girlhood may fade but sometimes,
I still hear the stars,
their voices against the dark
calling me home.

POMEGRANATE SEEDS & MISDEEDS

Softness is not a bad thing.
The world has enough sharp edges,
a deep rage where tenderness should live.

We need more kindness in this world.
More open hands and gentle voices that say,
"Stay because you matter."

We are taught to armor up and
to speak through a clenched jaw.
To flinch before we're even struck
as if caring makes us breakable.

So do not turn jaded. Love loudly.
Do not dim your light, let it shine.
Softness does not mean you're weak.
It means choosing peace in a society
that profits off of our pain.

LYRA WREN

I think I was born to give flowers
even if it leaves my garden empty.
To give more of myself than I'll ever get.
To offer what blooms in my chest,
even when the soil feels barren,
even when the petals fall too soon.

I give without thought of return,
because in the giving,
the world feels fuller
even if I stand here,
a little less than before.

POMEGRANATE SEEDS & MISDEEDS

I will make mistakes
and cry so loudly the earth shakes.

I will crush petals beneath my shaking fists
and drop them in surprise as if it was not my rage
that killed them in the first place.

I will mess up. I will keep messing up.
That is human and it's okay.
I'm learning.

This life has raised me up, loved me,
and left me crying on my knees.
It's embraced me and carried me
through the harder days.

It has carved me open and
planted grace in the wounds
like seeds in the cracks of stone.

There were moments I cursed it
and threw my hands to the sky
wondering *why*.

But then there were the tender moments,
when I held it like something sacred.
Fragile, imperfect but mine.

Section III:
Demeter Speaks

Demeter created a great many things
throughout her time on earth.
Golden fields of wheat that stretched
over the horizon line.

Vines that housed grapes her brother,
Dionysus, turned to wine.
At harvest time, the mortals plucked
the fruits of her labor as they prayed to her.

But by far, her greatest creation,
her dearest love, was Kore.

POMEGRANATE SEEDS & MISDEEDS

In the stillness before the wind,
Demeter cradles her newborn daughter.
She's a bloom not yet opened
and her breath is warm against her skin.

Kore stirs, fingers curling toward the light.
There is no sorrow here.
No Underworld waiting,
only the weightless beginning
of a story not yet spoken.

The earth holds its breath.
Even the stones listen as Demeter hums,
not a song but the shape of love
before it learns to grieve.

LYRA WREN

My sweet girl, with wildflowers in her hair
dancing around my gardens, carefree.
The sound of her laughter fills the air,
light as a breeze and soft as a prayer.

She runs around like a dream, barefoot and free.
Her spirit's a song in the hum of the trees.
In her eyes the world looks bright and new.
Every moment a gift and each step a truth.

I watch her, my little dancing girl
and time slips through my hands
like an hourglass with grains of sand.
I wonder how much longer I'll hold her near
before she dances on without me. Without fear.

POMEGRANATE SEEDS & MISDEEDS

Kore lies her head in her mother's lap
while the Goddess of Grain hums a soft lullaby
as if she were still a newborn.

Demeter weaves braids in her hair.
Tucking as many flowers as she can
into each set of strands.
She is the most nurturing of mothers,
caring for the land
as she cares for Kore.

Kore could have laid there forever,
just as her mother wanted
but even immortals must grow.

LYRA WREN

I taught the earth to bloom
and fed the world with my hands
but I could not keep my daughter safe.

She slipped beneath the earth
and the soil has never felt the same.

Each spring, I wait.
Not for flowers but for her footsteps.

POMEGRANATE SEEDS & MISDEEDS

When Kore was taken, I did not scream.
I let the earth speak for me.
Cracked soil, empty fields and
a silence that reached the gods.

Only a mother's grief could create winter.
Only a mother's love could bring life
back to a barren land.

Though Demeter knew of Zeus's power,
she bared her teeth still and
demanded the return of her daughter.

Mothers are fearless
when it comes to their children.
They are willing to face even gods
in order to protect them.

POMEGRANATE SEEDS & MISDEEDS

Let the mortals starve.
Let them hunger for the sun.
But until Kore returns
I will have them mourn
as I have done.

LYRA WREN

I am a mother before I am a god and
only a mother's love could threaten
to starve entire lands for her child's safe return.

So when Zeus tried to intimidate me
from his safe perch in the sky,
I told him only Kore's safe return
could have stopped me at that point.

POMEGRANATE SEEDS & MISDEEDS

For nine days, Demeter wandered earth
leaving a barren trail in her wake.
The fruits of her labor mottling.
Everywhere she went, it smelled like rotting.

She carried the torch until its fire
brushed the tips of her fingers
but she hardly felt the burn.

All she knew was an intense yearning:
to find her daughter,
the only home she'd ever really known.

LYRA WREN

I wait for your return
and listen for your voice
in every gust of wind.
My heart aches with each blossom I create.

You are the light in my hands,
the warmth in my chest
and the cold that shapes my grief.

Come back to me, Kore
even if only for a little while
so I can bloom once more.

The ground warms beneath her steps.
My daughter is home again.

Grief melts into green.
I touch the soil and it forgives me.

She was mine before the world
asked anything of her.
Before the Fates whispered
her name in the dark.

I fed her with my hands,
braided seasons in her hair.
She laughed like spring
before she ever knew winter.

Now she returns to me
shrouded in shadows like silk.
There is a softness in her I no longer know.

I love her still but my love
does not fit the woman she has become.

Demeter stared at Persephone upon
her return from the Underworld.
The cloying scent of flowers no longer
clung to her skin and her eyes didn't carry
the golden shine of summer's wheat
as they had been scorched by the flames of Hell.
Her daughter stood straight and
did not buckle beneath her gaze.

"Why was this not enough for you?"
Demeter gestured to the greenery
growing in the fields beneath her feet.

"Mama, I had to leave you as all daughters
must eventually do and once that
pomegranate juice stained my lips crimson, I knew.
I was wilting here but with Hades,"

Persephone smiled sadly at her mother
but her eyes had softened. "With him, I bloomed."

You've returned but not really.
Not to me.

The pomegranate bleeds
inside you still,
a red I cannot wash away.

"I just wanted to protect you,"
Demeter whispered, holding her daughter close.

"You did. You do.
But I'm not the same person anymore
and down there, I grew.
I am no longer a seedling and
I want to become a goddess
through my own means." Persephone replied.

The mother and child wept together
for both knew that they were changed.
That even if they desperately wanted to,
they could not remain in the past.

She walks to me, not as a daughter,
but as something made of both
endings and beginnings.

I no longer say the name
I once whispered into her hair.
Her hands no longer reach
for my apron or stories

But I accept her for what she is,
what she has become.
A queen of shadows and
a child of sunshine.

POMEGRANATE SEEDS & MISDEEDS

You are fearless, darling girl
and I hope you never forget it.
Even when you cannot be with me.
Even when you rule over cities of bone
in a world where things cannot grow.

I cannot promise I will not mourn
each time the earth splits and takes you with it.
But come each spring, I will welcome you home
as the flowers bloom, rejoicing in your return.

I don't know if my opinion holds much sway
but you are my daughter.
So I will accept you as both Kore and Persephone
because no matter what, in the end,
you will always be my baby.

Section IV:
The Mortal Grows

LYRA WREN

My mother gave birth to her rage and pain
and it carries my name.

POMEGRANATE SEEDS & MISDEEDS

I grew up in a house that threatened
to crack beneath my feet.
Carefully creeping around
because if I made a sound,
rage would burn it all down.
I don't know when it started
or why, just that I was a child
and my first steps were on eggshells.

The poison apple doesn't fall far
from the family tree
but how do I run from the blood
that flows through me?

My feet are frozen to the ground
and these roots are rotting swiftly.
I want to feel nourished by love
but I'm always left feeling empty.

Oh Mother, please tell me,
does a flower ever grow from a bad seed?

POMEGRANATE SEEDS & MISDEEDS

We are two tangled vines.
Roots that curl and fight for space
but still we are bound.

Some days we bloom
and some days we bruise
but always, we grow toward each other.

The little girl in me
learned to survive on crumbs.
She played pretend
that she was in a world
where violence looked like love.

The little girl inside of me
never believed she was enough.
She cries out for her parents still
but all she hears are echoes
and then a silence she can't fill.

POMEGRANATE SEEDS & MISDEEDS

I learned your voice
before I knew my own.
You spoke and the world suddenly made sense.

The names for things,
soft lullabies that lulled me to sleep.
Your words held me even when your arms were full.

Now I speak and sometimes I hear you
in the corners of my voice.
The tilt, the cadence, the way love shows up
without me having to say it.

There's a rhythm and a warmth
and even when you're not here,
I can still find you in my words.

To me, you were always just *mom*.
The one who watched over me
and encouraged me to grow.
The person who knew what everything was
and the one who made all the rules.

But now I see,
you were a whole person before I arrived.
A woman with dreams,
and regrets tucked quietly in drawers.
Stories I've never heard
and some you've never told.

You had a life before my name filled your days.
And somehow, you gave pieces of it away
so I could have my own.

What is it about a mother
that her chiding
makes my chest ache?

I still call out for her.
Even when I am hurting,
I am begging to be held.

Do you wish me to stay little and naive?
A soft girl who never gets angry.
A girl without claws and sharpened teeth
who leaves marks wherever she can reach.

I've made mistakes and hurt people
but I've learned from it too.
You cannot keep me sheltered forever,
tethered like a baby still in the womb.

I know the taste of dirt, shame and pain
so how could I stay the same?
Many times who I am has died
and I've been born again.

Sometimes I want to curl up in my mother's lap
just like I'm a little kid again.
I want her to brush my hair back
and tell me everything will be okay.

Somehow when *she* says it I believe her.
When I say it to myself, all I feel is doubt.

Girls have been leaving
their mothers behind for eons
Girls have been *taken*
from their mothers for longer.

POMEGRANATE SEEDS & MISDEEDS

To my mother,

How do I even begin to explain
that I want to spread my wings and fly
without making you feel left behind.

You put everything you had into raising me
and I know it will be hard for us when I leave.

Every baby born will one day flee the nest
but that doesn't make it any easier.
Even if it's for the best.

I am terrified of the rage
running through my blood
but my mother, with all her love,
always faces it head on.

She lets me scream and cry
and listens when I fall to my knees,
believing that I am lost and that
there is something wrong with me.

My mother shares my pain
and holds it as her own.
I think that's what motherhood is,
even when they've grown.

I am not a mother so I cannot imagine
how strange it must be to give birth to a being
that you get to call your own.
How you'd want them to be safe and sound,
so you surround them with four walls
and warm them with a mother's love.

How lost you must become when that baby is grown
and they decide it's time to leave home.

Demeter holds my face
in her motherly hands
as if I were her daughter.

She tells me that I matter.
That I would be missed if I was gone.
She says that it will be okay
and reminds me that I am strong.

She kisses my forehead gently
and encourages me to grow
and it is with her blessings
that I begin to bloom.

Section V:
Hades Speaks

When Hades was born he did not cry.
While Poseidon thrashed and Zeus lit the air with anger.
He came into the world silent, with eyes open,
dark like the spaces between stars.

The earth trembled,
not in fear but in recognition.
They wrapped him in shadow
not knowing they were giving him a kingdom.

He watched his mother, Rhea, weep.
Watched the sky close above her.
Already he understood that love and loss
were the same thing.

Hades did not choose the Underworld
but it fit him like a memory
he was born remembering.

POMEGRANATE SEEDS & MISDEEDS

I was devoured by Kronos
as soon as I was born.
And even when I escaped,
that echo of hunger followed me
everywhere I went.

I was ravenous for something
I could not touch.
What I craved beyond death
was something to fill the emptiness
of wanting to be loved.

While his brothers lounged in the clouds and sea,
darkness had been his destiny.

He ruled his realm with an iron fist
and though he was fair, he could be relentless.

This place, which was so dark and damp,
caused his ichor to run cold.

Hell could be a lonely place
even for the god who reigned in the Underworld.

The mortals fear me
and do not dare to breathe my name.
They call me Pluton, a giver of wealth,
as if they can escape their fate.

Nobody prays to the God of the Dead
until it is far too late.

I find it strange the way mortals
avoid saying my name.
Not asking me for favor until
they are condemned to my domain.

Fearing death will not save you from its claim.

POMEGRANATE SEEDS & MISDEEDS

Some thought me a monster
because I ruled over death.
As if death is cruel and
not a universal truth.

I do not drag these souls down,
they come to me: Mortals of all kinds.
Kings, peasants, lovers, and liars.
All equals in ash.

LYRA WREN

The mortals strike their palms
to the surface of the earth
in the hopes of invoking me.
As if I'm some spirit to summon
and not the pulse beneath their feet.

I am already there in your bone marrow,
already in the silence after the final word.

You build your fires
and chant your names
but I was never gone,
I've only ever waited.

Hades didn't know he was lonely.
Not really.

He just knew it was his duty
to keep order in the Underworld.

But sometimes, he watched the dead
reach for what they've lost,
and something within him ached
without a name.

Hades saw her standing there
with laughter lines and
wildflowers strewn in her hair.

And for the first time,
the God of Endings wanted a beginning.

POMEGRANATE SEEDS & MISDEEDS

She was undeniably beautiful
but that's not what drew me to her.
Kore watched the wilting flowers
with curiosity burning in her eyes.

This hurricane of spring
swept up the petals that burst beneath her feet
and stared as they crumpled to dust.

She held death so gently
brushing soft lips on its brow
then with ease brought it to life once more.

Hades wasn't the only one
who admired Kore
but he was the only one
who knew she deserved a throne.

LYRA WREN

Persephone, my sun,
like a flower I ache to be near you.

I find myself reaching for your warmth,
even down in the Underworld.
Only you could make this place a home.

POMEGRANATE SEEDS & MISDEEDS

Pressing starlit kisses
to the crown of my head,
you brought me to life
in the kingdom of the dead.

Pomegranate juice drips down your lips.
and when you smile,
blood stained teeth horrify
even the bravest of mortal men.

They do not see the glint in your eye
where darkness and light dance.

They do not know you hold death and life
in either hand.

The threads of fate have been woven and you're both,
the Queen of Hell and Goddess of Spring.
You're a contradiction. You're my everything.

"What do you think of when you think of Persephone?"
Hades asks the mortal.

"Honeysuckle, June, sunrises and dew."
They reply honestly.

"You think so?" He says with a wry smile, thinking back
to the wrath in her gaze when he crossed Persephone.
"Persephone isn't some delicate thing, you know.
She built a crown of thorn and bone
placing it on her head with bloodied hands.
When I think of Persephone I think of chaos and rust.
Strength and promise.
She is all you said but don't forget,
she holds life and death in either fist."

"Does death scare you?" Hades asks, his gaze steady.

The mortal looks into the shadows of his eyes
where the weight of countless souls are hidden.

"Yes," they admit. "But not in the way you think.
I fear the forgetting. The quiet that comes
when everything else fades away.
The moment when nobody is left to say your name."

He nods as if he has heard this answer a thousand times,
and in the silence the mortal wonders
if even the gods feel the same.

POMEGRANATE SEEDS & MISDEEDS

I was unmoved by most things.
The dead, the living, the gods of Olympus.

When Eurydice died by a snake's bite
and Orpheus cried that he must save his wife,
a resounding *no* echoed in my heart
even as he pleaded on his knees for my mercy.

Mortals died when they did
and this was no different.
But as he sang of love with his lyre
I looked over at Persephone
whose eyes had softened
and I could not deny her then.

Sometimes death is a girl in a night slip,
cheeks tinted pink from fever.
Or a soldier calling out for his mother
nearing his end in the battlefield.

Hades used to think death was unforgiving and cold
each time he heard mortals cry out as they mourned.
But when Hades watches Persephone kiss their foreheads
as their lips part on their last breath,
he thinks death has never looked so warm.

Section VI: The Mortal Grieves

The world loves a pretty dead girl.
One who cannot speak but is deemed
by other's voyeuristic tendencies.

"What a tragedy. She was so young," they say.
"Her beauty has been taken from us."
Even in death, they cannot escape.

I pity the pretty dead girls
I wish to take them by the hand
and reassure them that
I'll remember them for more than this.

I am swallowing down my grief
trying to get back to the girl I used to be.
But who was she?
And if I can't remember,
will I always feel this empty?

I'm so sorry for your loss
but I haven't lost anything.
It was ripped away from me.

The funeral is the hardest part
but what about the after?
The silence when everybody leaves.

They would have wanted you to go on
but there's no one here to tell me
how to keep breathing.

It will be okay
but it won't be because
they aren't here beside me.

POMEGRANATE SEEDS & MISDEEDS

I grieved while you were still alive
trying to make sure I could survive your passing
but nothing could have prepared me
for what losing you is like.

Where do I put the weight of my love for you?
How do I set it down?

My life has been irreversibly altered
and maybe even shattered.
But the world moved on
like it didn't even matter.

Some part of me wonders
if when people see me,
they can tell that I am changed.
That my life may never be the same.

Or is my face still a mirror
of the person they always knew.
Because for them,
there is no before and after.
It's just another day.
It's like nothing even happened.

Some days it's easy to forget
that you aren't here.
It always feels like you are just
in another room somewhere.
So I keep searching.
I can't seem to stop searching.
Even though I know you are gone.

There are claw marks on my grief
from how tightly I've held on.
It's all I have left of you.
How could I not?

With your last exhale,
I forgot how to breathe.
My whole world paused while
everyone else moved on around me

And yet, here I am
still holding my breath.

I think you took the air with you when you left.
I haven't taken a breath since you took your last.
It's caught in my chest and suffocates me.
How do I reach something I used to find with ease?

I think death makes us love more
because only when we've lost
do we realize our lasts.

The last time I heard your voice
or the last time we hugged.
Every last conversation that
dwindled late into the night.

With an ache that settles in my bones
I come to realize how much I'll miss.
The lost memories we would have made
if only you could have stayed.

"Come back to me in my dreams"
I want to plead but night after night
there's only silence it seems.

I reach for you in the dark,
but the space between us only grows
I hear echoes of your laughter,
faint as a memory too far away to hold.

But still each night I lie awake and plead
hoping for a dream where you return to me.

POMEGRANATE SEEDS & MISDEEDS

We begin to die the moment we are born
but the gods, they live forever.
Their stories get passed down
and their epithets are spoken in reverence.

I wonder if I gift you eternity
each time your name crosses my lips.
I'll speak of you for the rest of my days
so please, stand by my side and stay.

There is more beyond the grave,
like sweet reunion and new beginnings.
Where the soul, once filled with longing,
finds its rest in familiar arms.

There, I'll run to you once more,
no goodbyes left to fear.

Time no longer tethers us
and distance is a forgotten word.
It's a life that never ends even when
I exhale my last breath.

POMEGRANATE SEEDS & MISDEEDS

Grief is many things but for me
it was so quiet that one could hear
the echoes of laughter left behind.

An unbearable absence lingered heavy
in my chest that no feeling could fill.
I didn't really know how to exist in a
world without you in it but somehow
each day I was growing around my anguish
until the emptiness didn't feel quite so heavy.

Some days I can barely breathe but more often
there are times that I can smile and laugh.
I don't think this hurt will ever go away
but I take comfort in knowing I must
have loved you a lot to feel this raw.

When you choose to love someone
you make a vow with the universe,
an unspoken promise that one day
this love is going to cause you pain.

Because to know love, is to know grief.
To say hello, you will one day have to
say goodbye. When it hurts love feels
like a curse and I wonder why I would
subject myself to this misery but by gods,
if it isn't worth it every time.

Hades and Persephone,

May you watch over my loved ones
who have faded away
May you embrace me when I miss them
and help to keep them safe.

Let your darkness be soft.
Let your silence be kind.
Hold them close as I would,
if I still could.

Death finds a way to strip you bare.
There are no lies to hide behind,
no masks or pretenses.
Only the raw truth of what remains
when everything else has faded.

In this moment,
there is nothing left to prove.
Only the soft surrender of all that you were
and the peace of what stays.

POMEGRANATE SEEDS & MISDEEDS

When I die, return my body to the earth
and let the flowers grow from my rotting corpse.
Let my eternity live in the petals
that blow so gently in the breeze.

Do not stand over my grave and weep
for something beautiful blooms in this death.

When I die, do not mourn me.
My spirit flows through the wind and trees.
You will find me near the flowers each spring,
alongside Persephone.

I will rise in the scent of the damp earth,
in the hush before blossoms break open.
I will drift through the branches like a breath
and tangle myself in the golden hairs of dandelions.

Look for me where light softens the soil,
where seeds brave the dark for a chance to bloom.
I do not vanish. I return, again and again,
with the turning of the world.

Let your sorrow fall like rain
then watch how gently I grow from it.

POMEGRANATE SEEDS & MISDEEDS

Section VII:
Persephone and the Poet

I understand you, Persephone.
We too mix our godhood with girlhood.
Despite our divinity, we are just as hungry.

POMEGRANATE SEEDS & MISDEEDS

Am I more Persephone or Kore?
Can I have one without the other?

A daughter of flowers
and harbinger of death.
Some days I am petals.
Others, I am ash.

There is beauty in my duality
and a strength in holding all of me.
Even the parts I once tried to hide,
are asking gently to be seen.

You're standing at the threshold
and I know that place so well.

The moment before you fall,
it feels like you're breaking
but in truth, you're tearing down the walls.

Go. This darkness will not unmake you.
It will teach you your name.

POMEGRANATE SEEDS & MISDEEDS

You fear the dark
as if it means the end.
I once did, too.

I have danced in both worlds
and held death like a lover.

So when the night comes for you,
do not tremble.

There are flowers even here.

Even the gods,
with all their divine shrouds
of marble and distance,
have sat with their own undoing.

Even they have looked
into the eyes of mortals
wanting to be understood
without laurels and worship.

I am the Queen of the Underworld,
born of pomegranate seeds and deceit,
but I am also a child of loss.

So when you call my name,
do not clutch it like a prayer.

Meet me, not just as a goddess
and Queen of the Dead,
but as a girl who chose the dark
in search of her own light.

POMEGRANATE SEEDS & MISDEEDS

You want only the sweet things.
The soft days, the clean pages,
the version of you that doesn't ache.

But growth doesn't ask for your comfort.
It asks for your surrender.

Eat the fruit.
Let it stain your mouth.
Know yourself in every flavor
even when it's bitter.

There is something holy
in learning to hold your own sorrow
without flinching.

So have the courage to keep tasting life.
Even when it hurts.

I live in both a garden and a grave.
I carry spring in my breath
and winter within my bones.

You too, can hold both.
Grieve what you've lost
and then grow from it.

I watch Persephone as her hands
weave through the air,
flowers floating off her fingertips.

"You create all this beauty
just for it to die." I say quietly.

"Does that mean it was not worth the time?"
Persephone replies with a soft smile.

"Living things are not eternal.
Yes, they will die but come next spring,
they will blossom again. Such is the way of life."

She hands me a narcissus which I cradle in my hands
I know it will die but I hold it to my cheek and smile.
Until then, I will cherish it.

I carry her story
like a secret pressed between my ribs
and listen as Persephone whispers
"They thought taking me would end me
but I chose to rise in the darkness, blazing."

I want to tell her that I know.
That I, too, have lived
between versions of myself,
calling it survival.

They call it myth
but I call it memory.
Because I've stood in the slow unspooling
of who I was and what I was becoming.

Her story is mine, too.
I've gone through hell and
emerged on the other side changed.
But I've discovered my power
in the pieces of myself that have remained.

In the end,
Persephone takes me by the hand and
quietly leads me to the edges of her mother's meadow.

I came here looking for answers.
I wanted to make sense of this hunger
that bloomed from deep within me.

"They think I was stolen," Persephone says.
"But I stayed. Not because I had to but because I changed.
I did something with the darkness that tried to unmake me."

"I want, Persephone. I want so deeply
that it scares me." I reply with tears in my eyes.

"You're not broken for wanting." She smiles.
"You're becoming all that you were meant to be
and you can be more than just one thing.
Hunger only means you are still alive enough to grow."

She lets go of my hand, not a dismissal but a blessing.
She watches as I walk back through the meadow,
the soil soft beneath my feet,
carrying nothing but myself which,
for the first time, feels like enough.

Special Acknowledgments

- *Thank you to my mom* who constantly inspires me, pushes me to follow my dreams and listens to me on my worst and best days.

- *Thank you to my dad* for supporting me in this journey wholeheartedly and for always encouraging me to pursue my creative ideas.

- *Thank you to my sisters* for always having my back and supporting me in every creative endeavor I pursue.

- *Thank you to Keller* for never complaining when I send you hundreds of new poems and for taking care to design each new book I send you.

- *Thank you to my best friends and family* who always encourage me and are the first to buy my books.

- *Thank you to Maddie* for editing this book and making sure it came out looking polished.

- *Thank you to my followers and readers,* I couldn't do this without all of you encouraging me and reminding me why I write. To bring comfort, compassion and understanding to my audience. You make me feel loved and heard. I hope I make you feel the same way.

About The Author

Lyra Wren is a poet and storyteller born and raised in Indiana. She's been a creative ever since she was a little girl whether that was doodling in the empty spaces of her homework or writing countless stories for her family to read. She has a Bachelor's degree in Studio Art at Indiana University. When she isn't writing in the cafe of her local bookstore, Lyra spends much of her time painting, reading, enjoying the outdoors, curating spotify playlists and perusing astrological charts.

In 2021, Lyra began posting her poetry to TikTok and she has since grown her online following into a large supportive community. She strives to bring comfort, hope and understanding to her audience and make the world a place where people feel a bit less alone.

 *@poetrybylyra*

@canned.spaghettio

About The Book

In this lyrical collection, the myth of Persephone
is cracked open and retold from the inside out
through the eyes of Persephone, Demeter, Hades
and the poet herself.

These poems speak not of abduction, but of agency.
Not of silence, but of voice.

Blending ancient myth with modern femininity,
Pomegranate Seeds and Misdeeds is a reclamation
of power and a conversation between Persephone
and every woman who's ever been told
to stay soft, to stay small and to stay silent.

Also by Lyra Wren

The Lost Girls takes readers through the ups and downs of life.

This book is a collection of poems reminding people
to find joy in the journey and the little things.

It reminds us to engage with our emotions even when it hurts.

That life is about discovery and rediscovery
and that it's normal to feel lost.

Finding beauty in the day to day,
even when things feel adrift,
is a tremendous power.

Fireflies are not stars but it's still okay for us
to dream on them anyway.

(Cover and book design by Keller Makemson.)

Praise for *The Lost Girls*

"It's like lyra wren was able to bring out all of my thoughts in the most beautiful spot on way.

Allowing us to realize we are not alone with our feelings and experiences. This set of poetry helps you look into a scramble mind in a lovely manner.

A must read to understand one another."

– LienRenders

"This is one of the most beautiful and creative poetry collections i've ever read. i'm convinced she crawled inside of my brain and wrote down all of my thoughts then made poems out of it. i don't have the right words to explain how breathtaking this book is."

– Mae Setrova

"It's not an easy feat to tackle big topics in short-form writing and poetry, but Lyra is so talented... I highly recommend The Lost Girls to all women, all readers who care about women, and anyone who likes poetry...I will definitely be rereading this collection, and sharing more of Lyra's work in the future."

– Hayley

The Stars that Knew You is a collection of poetry touching on sisterhood and the curious complexities it brings. Lyra dives into the heart of what being a sister means: the ways in which they know you, humble you and inspire you all in one breath. Many people will come and go but they are the only ones who will stick with you for a lifetime.

"My sister and I were lying side by side
beneath the moonlight when she softly said,

'If you told me the stars knew you
by name, I would believe you.'

'I think if they knew anyone's name,
it would be yours.' I replied.

She wrinkled her nose in confusion
before quietly asking, 'Why?'

'Because all I ever do is speak of you.' "

(Cover and book design by Keller Makemson.)

Praise for *The Stars That Knew You*

"This book really was a cute find I just bought it because of the title it sounded sweet and I love poem books, then when it came I realized it was for older daughters who have sisters and it was just so fitting because I'm the oldest daughter of 4 girls so it definitely spoke to me! Some of the poems brought me to tears and I love a book that can do that!"

– Elena Reyes

"Cried from the first page to the last page. Such a well written book! It was really something anybody with siblings could relate to. I can't recommend it enough."

– Natalie Perez

"Sobbed my way through this. Such an amazing collection of poetry that is so relatable and takes me back to my childhood."

– Hayley (Shelflyfe)